Working Paper 13-1 — "Distressed Sales and the FHFA House Price Index"
Executive Summary (E.S.)

E.S.I   Introduction

Since the beginning of the housing bust, a significant share of real estate transactions across the country have been "distressed" sales. Such transactions include sales of bank-owned properties—also known as Real Estate Owned (REO) sales—and "short" sales. The latter are situations where borrowers sell their properties for less than the outstanding mortgage balance and banks agree to accept the proceeds as payment in full for the outstanding loan.

FHFA has produced a Working Paper that evaluates distressed sales and studies their impact on house price indexes. "Distressed Sales and the FHFA House Price Index,"[1] uses real estate transaction data from the state of Florida to address three basic questions:

1. To what extent have distressed sales had an influence on the measured house price trends?

2. Is the methodology FHFA currently uses for identifying—and removing—distressed sales from its "distress-free" indexes reliable?

3. How can price discounts associated with distressed sales be tracked over time and how large have such discounts been?

This Executive Summary provides a brief overview of the paper's research findings in these three areas.

E.S.II   Influence of Distressed Sales on Measurements of House Prices

For reasons detailed in prior FHFA publications,[2] homes sold in distress tend to sell at significant discounts relative to other transactions. Given this discount, even without looking at the empirical data, it would be reasonable to assume that such sales would have a significant impact on aggregate measurements of home price trends. For instance, price changes reflected in house price indexes, such as FHFA's House Price Index (HPI),[3] should be influenced by the number of and discount associated with such sales.

By comparing FHFA's standard house price indexes—which incorporate sales price data from short sales and REO transactions—to FHFA's "distress-free" indexes (which remove such sales from the underlying data sample)—this Working Paper confirms that distressed sales have had a significant effect on the FHFA HPI. Focusing on price measures for Miami and Tampa, Florida, the paper reveals that FHFA's distress-free indexes showed more modest price declines than FHFA's standard price indexes during the early part of the housing bust. In other words, the presence of

---

[1]The paper available at http://www.fhfa.gov/PolicyProgramsResearch/Research/Pages/Working-Paper-13-1.aspx.

[2]See Mortgage Market Note 12-01, "A Primer on Price Discount of Real Estate Owned (REO) Properties" available at http://www.fhfa.gov/PolicyProgramsResearch/Research/Pages/Mortgage-Market-Note-12-01.aspx.

[3]FHFA's HPI is a "repeat sales" house price index formed from mortgage data supplied by Fannie Mae and Freddie Mac. Details about underlying methodology at www.fhfa.gov/PolicyProgramsResearch/Research/Pages/HPI-Technical-Description.aspx.

distressed sales in the standard HPI had a depressing effect on measured price changes. In more recent periods, when distressed sales comprised a shrinking percentage of real estate transactions, the Working Paper reveals the opposite effect. As the "weight" of distressed sales on the standard index decreased in recent periods, the depressing effect lessened over time. This meant that the price appreciation observed in the standard FHFA index was somewhat above what the distress-free measures reported.

Figure E.S.1: HPI Trends—Purchase-Only vs. Distress-Free Price Indexes

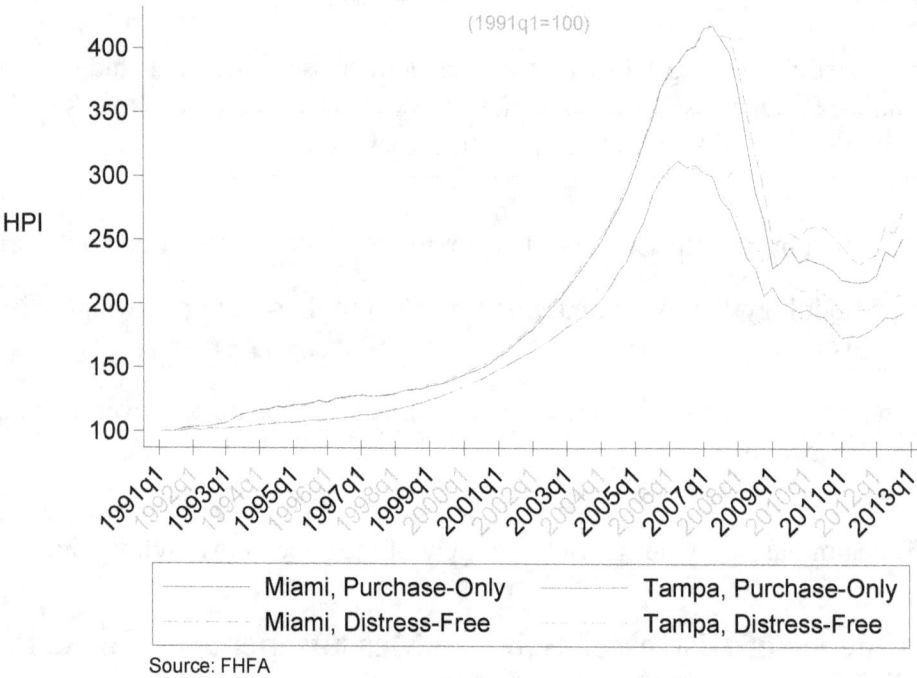

Source: FHFA

By comparing the standard and distress-free indexes over the last several years, Figure E.S.1 reveals the impact that distressed sales had on measured price changes in recent periods. Though data limitations preclude the identification of many distressed sales in early periods (e.g., the early 1990s), the figure clearly shows very large differences between the standard and distress-free house price indexes in recent years.

E.S.III Identifying Distressed Sales

Having confirmed that distressed sales have had a substantial impact on measured price trends, the Working Paper then sets out to evaluate whether FHFA's approach to identifying distressed sales is reasonable. Testing the reliability of the approach is important because it is generally not possible to know with certainty whether a given real estate transaction is a distressed sale. In some cases—situations where a sale involved a bank-owned property—county recorder data can be used to make relatively strong inferences. Short sales are much more difficult to identify, however, and inferences can be made with less certainty.

To test whether FHFA's method for making inferences is reliable, the Working Paper looks at county assessor data obtained from the state of Florida. For a large set of historical property transactions in that state, county assessors have made their own determinations as to whether particular sales were distressed or not.[4] For thousands of individual transactions, the Working Paper looks at whether FHFA's distressed sale inference agrees with the inference made by the county assessor offices.

In a significant proportion of cases, concurrence was found between FHFA's inference and that of the assessor office; in other words, a sale was identified as "distressed" or "nondistressed" by both FHFA and the assessor office. For 25 to 35 percent of recent transactions, however, no such concurrence existed. Either FHFA indicated that the sale was distressed and the assessor disagreed or, vice-versa—the assessor indicated distressed while FHFA did not. In analyzing these cases where there is "disagreement," the Working Paper found strong evidence that the FHFA methodology provides a reliable indication of distress.

The evidence comes in the form of systematic differences in price appreciation. In cases where FHFA indicated that a transaction was distressed but the assessor office indicated otherwise, the average selling prices were found to be lower than would be expected for traditional (nondistressed) transactions. Given that distressed sales typically involve significant price discounts, this meant that the FHFA-identified distressed sales "looked" very much like distressed sales. Conversely, in cases where the Florida assessors indicated distressed but FHFA did not, average selling prices often were not substantially lower than would be expected. Small—and in some cases nonexistent—discounts for such transactions suggested that many of those cases may not have been actual distressed sales.

E.S.IV   Distressed Sale Discount

The Working Paper also evaluates how distressed sale discounts have varied over time in Florida. The paper describes a simple methodology for estimating the average size of discount and the average discount during specific time periods. The methodology involves a minor adjustment to the basic house price model used for forming the FHFA House Price Index. The approach is valuable because it is easy to implement and because time series information about distressed discounts is very difficult to find; typically, only anecdotal information for such discounts is available in the public domain.

Figure E.S.2 reports the historical discounts calculated by the Working Paper for the state of Florida. Across the roughly 20 years between 1994 and 2013, the Working Paper estimated that the average price discount was about 14 percent, but the discount varied significantly across years. In the late 1990s, for example, the discount tended to be between 10-15 percent. As the housing boom accelerated, the discount shrank significantly to between 5 and 10 percent and some periods even saw discounts of less than 5 percent. Immediately thereafter, during the early part of the housing bust (roughly 2007 to 2010), the discount rose sharply to near 30 percent. In recent quarters, with the onset of the recovery and rising home prices, such discounts have become slightly more modest. In the first quarter of 2013, for instance, the average discount was about 25 percent.

---

[4]Assessors make the determination in the process of forming assessed values for individual properties. Prices for distressed sales are generally not to be used in deriving estimates of home values.

Figure E.S.2: Distressed Sale Discount in Florida—By Quarter

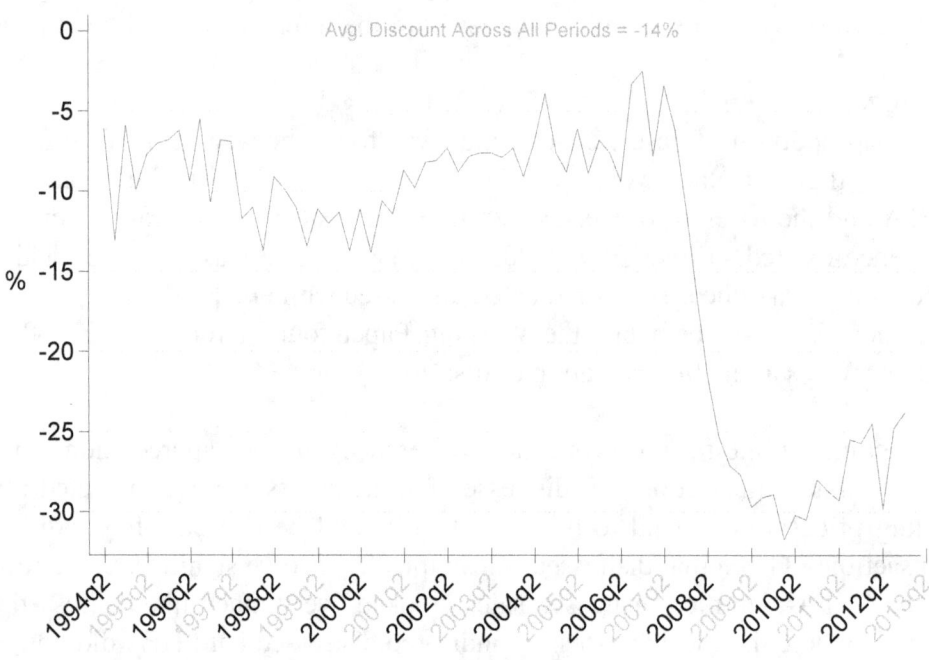

Sources: FHFA, DataQuick Information Systems, FHA, and CoreLogic

E.S.V   Conclusion

Until the onset of the housing bust, distressed sales comprised a relatively trivial proportion of the data used to construct FHFA's House Price Index. When coupled with the fact that distressed sales were priced at very modest and relatively stable price discounts relative to other property transactions, the small share meant that there was limited demand for price measures that were not directly influenced by such transaction.

As the housing bust developed and demand for such measures increased, FHFA responded with the release of distress-free house price indexes in the summer of 2012. The analysis in the Working Paper suggests that, although the measures are still relatively new, they are founded on a reliable methodology. The analysis also indicates that price discounts associated with distressed sales can be easily measured. Using a newly-developed approach to measuring the trends, the paper shows significant variations over time in the magnitude of such discounts in the state of Florida.

Although housing markets are strengthening, short sales and sales of bank-owned properties likely will continue to play a significant role in housing markets in the near future. FHFA will continue to study such transactions and, in its efforts to provide the public with more and better information on market conditions, related follow-up analyses may be published in future Working Papers, Mortgage Market Notes, or HPI news releases. Questions about current or future research on distressed sales and, more generally, house prices can be addressed to HPIHelpDesk@fhfa.gov.

I   Introduction

Distressed sales (sales of REO and short sales) have comprised a significant share of real estate transactions since the start of the housing bust. Distressed sales differ from traditional or arms-length transactions in several ways that affect asset valuations. For instance, they may come with significant discounts because of extra-motivated sellers. Distressed sales also are discounted, at times, because of quality-related problems (FHFA 2012c). Not surprisingly, in the context of tracking real estate values with price indexes, such sales can have a non-trivial effect on measured price changes. Removing such sales from the full sample and re-estimating a "distress-free" set of metrics can produce different estimates of short- and medium-run price changes than are reflected in the standard index where distressed sales are included but not identified. The gap between the measured price change estimates reflects the fact that: (a) the share of distressed sales varies over time and (b) the discount associated with distressed sales is large and not fixed.

This paper begins by comparing the Federal Housing Finance Agency's (FHFA) standard index against the newly released "distress-free" index approach (FHFA 2012a). The analysis shows sizeable deviations in recent periods. In short, distressed sales matter a great deal to index estimates. Next, the paper attempts to validate FHFA's current approach to identifying distressed sales. Identifying such sales is not a straightforward exercise and, while FHFA believes that its current approach is reasonable, no approach is perfect. Employing an outside data source from the Florida Department of Revenue (FDOR), the analysis studies the consistency with which FHFA's approach aligns with distressed sales identifications made by county assessors. At least in Florida, there is strong evidence for the reliability of FHFA's current approach. Finally, the paper studies the discounts associated with real estate owned (REO) and short sales. A simple approach to measuring the impact of distressed sales on index valuations is discussed and we report the empirically estimated magnitudes of such discounts. A discussion and conclusion follow.

II   Comparing Standard and Distress-Free Indexes

This year marks the fiftieth anniversary of the seminal work where Bailey et al. (1963) define a statistical technique to measure house price changes in real estate markets. The estimation—dubbed a repeat sales method—requires limited data about sales transactions and avoids the need for actual characteristics or details of the properties. The methodology produces more stable and lower index estimates than the previously used chain method. Further studies have since refined and popularized the repeat sales method (see Case & Shiller 1987, 1989). Other classic works have tried to steer the literature away from repeat sales and toward hedonic approaches (Rosen 1974). This line of applied work questions whether benefits from property characteristics are internalized in house prices (Linneman 1980), considers how the marginal values of property characteristics differ across regions (Sirmans et al. 2006), and, more recently, even applies the hedonic approaches to create land price indexes (Sirmans & Slade 2012). Alternatives to the repeat sales approach certainly exist (Gatzlaff & Ling 1994; Noeth & Sengupta 2011); however, the simplicity and minimal data requirements have established it as a leading method for measuring housing market trends.

As part of its regulatory role in the housing finance system, the FHFA has been producing house price indexes (HPIs) using a repeat sales approach since March 1996.[1] Three versions of the HPI are published: the "purchase-only", "all-transactions", and "expanded-data" indexes. The sole distinction between the different versions is the underlying data samples used for index estimation.[2] Within the different versions of the HPI, separate indexes are calculated for various geographic areas (nationwide, census divisions, states, and metropolitan areas). All of these HPIs and fla-

---

[1]FHFA was established in 2008 by combining the Federal Housing Finance Board (FHFB), the Office of Federal Housing Enterprise Oversight (OFHEO), and the government-sponsored enterprise mission office at the U.S. Department of Housing and Urban Development. Earlier reports were published under the OFHEO agency name.

[2]The purchase-only index uses sales price information from single-family, purchase-money mortgages acquired or guaranteed by Fannie Mae and Freddie Mac. The all-transactions index increases the sample by including appraisal values from refinance mortgages acquired or guaranteed by the Enterprises. The expanded-data index begins with the dataset used for estimating the purchase-only index and adds two additional data sources: sales price data for houses with mortgages endorsed by the Federal Housing Administration and real property county recorder data licensed from DataQuick.

vors employ a weighted, repeat sales methodology that measures average price changes in repeat transactions on the same properties (for statistical details, refer to Calhoun 1996).

Recently, FHFA has begun publishing a distress-free HPI as an offshoot of its purchase-only suite of indexes. The new index is estimated with a dataset that does not include distressed sales. To identify and remove distressed sales, FHFA uses mortgage performance data, deed data, and pre-foreclosure records. A transaction is considered "distressed" in cases where at least one of the three data sources indicates some type of distress.

The first of the three data sources, mortgage performance data, includes information on the payment and delinquency status of loans guaranteed by Fannie Mae and Freddie Mac (hereafter called the "Enterprises") or endorsed by the Federal Housing Administration (FHA). A sales transaction is labeled as distressed if the Enterprise or FHA payment data indicate that the seller was delinquent by two or more months some time in the preceding twelve months.[3] The second of the three data sources, deed data from county recorder offices, is licensed from DataQuick Information systems. A sales transaction is considered distressed if the deed data indicate that the bank or mortgagee took over the property during the preceding year. Such transfers are associated with the recording of certain deed types and other documents, including Trustee Deeds upon Sale, Foreclosure Deeds, Sheriff's Deed, and Certificates of Final Judgment. The third and final dataset used for identifying distressed sales entails preforeclosure data licensed from CoreLogic. These data, which are particularly useful where the seller does not have an Enterprise or FHA-endorsed mortgage (i.e., where mortgage performance data are unavailable to FHFA), include public notices of borrower distress. These records include Notices of Default and Lis Pendens filings. Such filings reflect the early stage of the foreclosure process and signal borrowers who have been late on their payments. To summarize, if any of the three datasets (mortgage performance data, deed data, and preforeclosure records) contains a flag then the property transaction is labeled with the distressed sale indicator.

---

[3]A property is not flagged if it sells at some point between the current sale date and the delinquency period.

Figure 1: HPI Trends Over Time: Purchase-Only versus Distress-Free

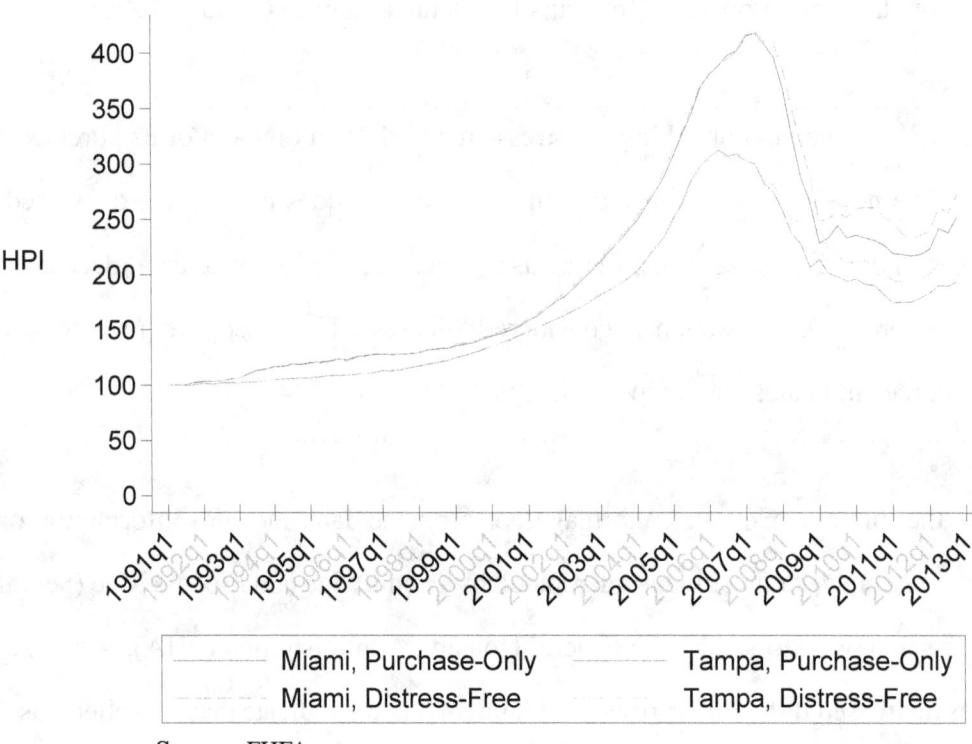

Source: FHFA.

Using the various internal and external data sources to identify and remove distress sales, distress-free HPIs are created with the same repeat sales methodology as is used to estimate the standard purchase-only indexes. Figure 1 offers a visual comparison of the standard purchase-only and distress-free indexes for two metro areas in Florida. All of the data are computed quarterly and seasonally adjusted. The seasonally adjusted purchase-only HPIs follow similar trends: they increase dramatically in the early 2000s, peak at the end of 2006 or start of 2007, and drop sharply until 2009. The HPIs are relatively stagnant for several years until they begin to rise again at the start of 2012. For both metro areas, the distress-free indexes mimic the full-sample, purchase-only index until the housing market crash when the purchase-only indexes fall more than the distress-free indexes. In Tampa, the purchase-only index level drops further but the quarterly changes of both indexes appear relatively similar starting in 2009. The story is not the same in Miami where the distress-free index stabilizes for several quarters. These graphical examples suggest that distressed transactions tend to depress index estimations and that appreciation/depreciation rates may vary over time and between geographic areas. Clearly, there is a visual difference between the two types of indexes after the housing boom. The next section addresses the validation of the distressed sale flags.

III Validating How Distressed Sales Are Flagged

No collection of data sources—not even the combination of proprietary and supervisory data assembled by FHFA—will perfectly identify all distressed sales. Identifying such transactions is difficult because it requires property-level information about loan payment status and accurate mapping of court records to property databases.[4] An alternative approach to identifying distressed sales would be to use indicators from county assessor offices. In determining property values, county assessors use sales data and, in many places, are instructed to avoid using distressed sales in their determinations. Tax roll data—which most places are public information—often report recent sales and, in some locations, indicate whether those recent sales were distressed. In this paper, we use transactions data from Florida.

Florida is a disclosure state that provides a wealth of longitudinal real estate data, including indications of whether property sales were distressed. Annual county tax rolls are collected and standardized by the FDOR for regulatory oversight.[5] After combining county tax rolls, any property across the state can be studied based on its location or permitted land use.[6] Additional details offer the price, date, and a "qualification code" for each property transaction. This qualification code identifies arms-length transactions and, importantly for this analysis, also flags distressed

---

[4]Two FHFA Quarterly Highlights Pieces have been devoted to the inherent challenges with creating a distress-free index (2012a; 2012b).

[5]Data are collected by their Property Tax Oversight Program and are posted annually at ftp://sdrftp03.dor.state.fl.us/Tax%20Roll%20Data%20Files/. The DeVoe Moore Center at Florida State University has collected and preserved historical records beyond what is currently maintained by the FDOR.

[6]Forming this database is not a simple task. County tax rolls are available from 1995 to 2012 for the state's 67 counties, representing over 162 million property-year observations. Specific details can be provided upon request but, in short, the two most recent transactions are stacked across counties, appended over years, and observations are dropped where information is missing, duplicated, or updated later. The result is a statewide database of approximately 13.8 million sales from 1970 until 2012. Nearly three-fifths the sales are single-family residential properties.

sales.[7]

To compare the distress indicators produced by FHFA and those reflected in the FDOR data, addresses are standardized and the two datasets are merged together.[8] Perfect matches are kept—where sales information and distressed sales indicators are in both databases—and reflect 1.4 million single-family sales transactions from 1975 through 2012 across Florida. How do the distressed sales indicators compare between the datasets? Figure 2 splits the question into two parts by displaying the fraction of flagged sales and the overlaps between the datasets.

Panel (a) shows the share of distressed sales (out of the full sample of residential transactions) began rising at the end of 2007 and reached a local peak in 2009. This is not a surprise given that asset prices were riskier and defaults higher at the end of the housing boom and leading into the bust period. As the legend conveys, the bars are split into three groups as the share of distressed sales from the FDOR's public assessor records, the FHFA proprietary data from the Enterprises, and the FHFA data combined with private datasets for mortgage performance, deeds, and preforeclosure flags. The FDOR dataset's bars do not begin until the first quarter of 2009 because that was the first year when the FDOR's qualification codes began identifying distressed sales. All three bars follow a similar pattern until the third quarter of 2009 when FHFA shows higher increases in distressed sales.

Two important takeaways emerge from this graph. First, the FHFA data indicate an average share of at least 11 percent more distressed sales than the FDOR public data. Second, the FHFA proprietary data flags are supplemented in material ways by the preforeclosure data licensed from

[7]Before 2009, the FDOR sales qualification codes took on only four values with the lowest value representing a qualified sale but none of the codes indicated a distressed sale. In 2009 and 2010, the FDOR expanded the codes with greater detail. Distressed sales are sales with corrective deeds, quite claims, or tax deeds; deeds to or from financial institutions; sales under extreme circumstances like a forced sale or duress sale; and a sale to prevent foreclosure.

[8]A combination of merges are done based on the property's CBSA, physical address, sale year, sale month, and sale price with the FHFA database being the master dataset. The final match rate for merging onto the FHFA dataset is 87 percent across the state with 92 percent in Miami and 90 percent in the Tampa.

Figure 2: Comparing Distressed Sales in Florida

(a) Shares of the Datasets Indicating Distressed Sales

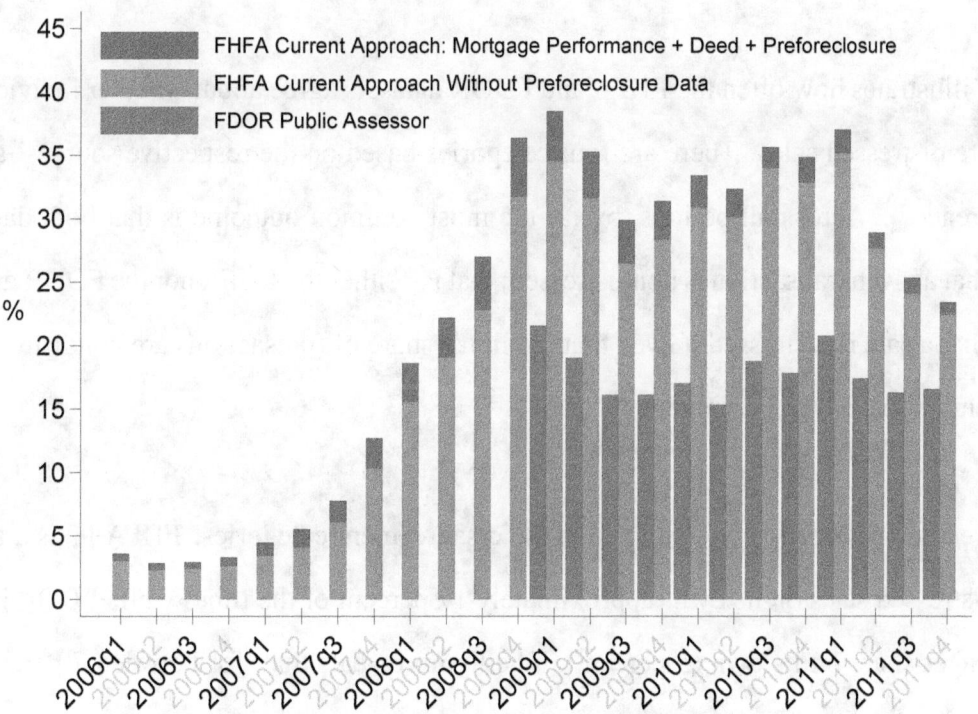

Sources: FHFA, DataQuick Information Systems, FHA, and CoreLogic.

(b) Concurrence of Distress Identifiers between Datasets

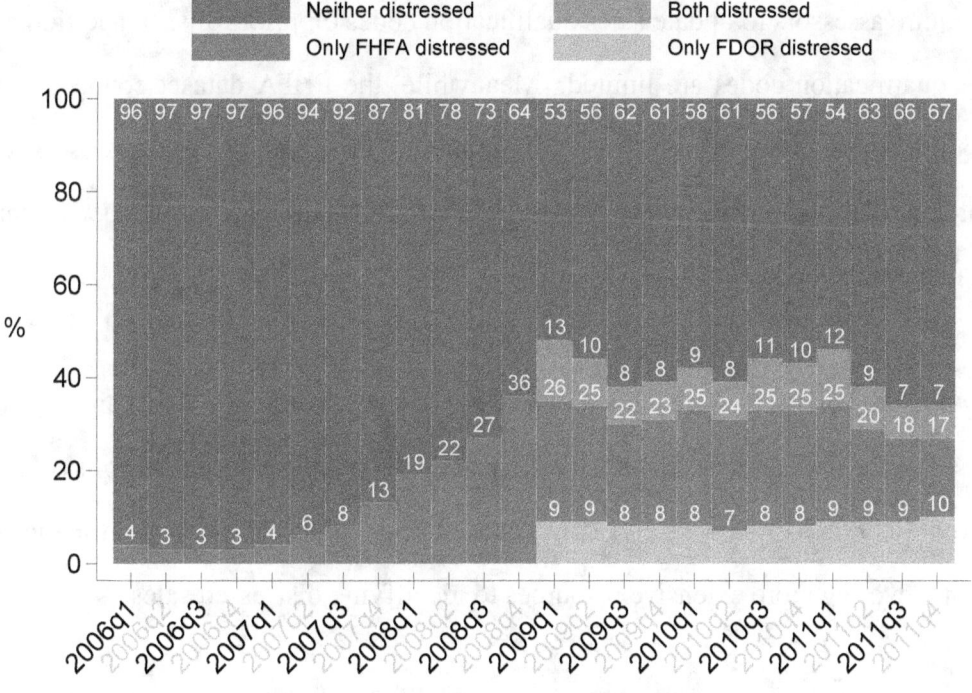

Sources: FHFA, DataQuick Information Systems, FHA, and CoreLogic.

CoreLogic. The preforeclosure data, which was first licensed in 2012, increases the estimated share of distressed sales by several percentage points in each quarter.

Panel (b) illustrates how often the FHFA and FDOR datasets agree about whether individual transactions are distressed sales. There are four categories based on the respective sources' agreement ("concurrence"). Across all periods, by far the most common outcome is that both data sources suggest that a given transaction is nondistressed; that is neither the FHFA nor the FDOR approaches suggest that a sale is distressed. Given that the lion's share of transactions are nondistressed transactions, this overlap is not surprising.

The interesting information is contained in the disagreement categories. FHFA finds a large fraction of distressed sales on its own (approximately 17 percent of the time) while FDOR indicates a more meager share on its own (5 percent). The figure reveals that, for between 7 percent and 13 percent of transactions, the FDOR and FHFA approaches both agree on a sale being distressed.

Why might the two sources disagree? The county tax rolls are static snapshots and the FDOR does not require assessors to update sales qualification codes on prior rolls. In addition, the quality checks for qualification codes are limited. Meanwhile, the FHFA dataset connects loan performance, county records, and preforeclosure information to prior sales. While assessors have access to some of these data, they do not have access to direct information about loan performance. Also, their data may not be updated.

Assuming that the FHFA-identified distressed sales are truly distressed sales, Panel (b) reveals that less than half of the total distressed sales are flagged by the public assessor tax rolls (i.e., the FDOR data). Given this relatively low rate of agreement, it seems that the assessment authorities might benefit from devoting more extensive resources to identifying distressed sales.

IV Quantifying the Magnitude of the Distressed Sale Discount

The impact of distressed sales on house price valuations is a relatively new but quickly developing topic among researchers. Studies have used hedonic, repeat sale, and propensity score matching methods to measure the negative impacts on prices. An often cited study, Immergluck & Smith (2006), finds a 10 percent house value decline during 1997 and 1998 in Chicago. Campbell et al. (2011) measures the foreclosure discount to be 27 percent in Massachusetts with data from 1987 to 2009. Both studies agree that foreclosures diminish the values of nearby houses. Concentrations of foreclosures also increase the likelihood of other foreclosures leading up to or during the housing market crash (see Harding et al. (2009, 2012); Towe & Lawley (2013)). These studies, though, focus on the impact to individual asset prices and not the valuation for a group of assets, like captured by a HPI. Furthermore, the impact of distressed sales may be more pronounced after the market crash—a period not covered by the literature. The choice between a traditional purchase-only and distress-free HPI, thus, has grown more relevant as housing markets stabilize and recover.

As shown in the last section, the FHFA and FDOR distressed sale indicators do not always concur. Although the FHFA indicators identify more transactions as being distressed, this does not mean necessarily that approach has better accuracy. Because the literature finds that distressed properties sell consistently below prices for nondistressed properties, a reasonable comparison is between observed price trends where the two approaches disagree. For example, in cases where FHFA alone identifies a recent transaction as distressed, a pertinent question is, "Is the observed appreciation for that property less than would be expected?" Since an actual distressed sale should exhibit lower-than-average price appreciation (or greater price depreciation), the relative appreciation provides indirect evidence about the accuracy of the identification methodology. A lower-than-average appreciation would provide confirmation that identified distressed sales are truly distressed sales.

Relating this notion back to the repeat sales regression methodology, the issue is whether the

Table 1: Average Regression Errors for Transactions with Disagreement in Distress Identifiers

	Assessor: Non-distressed FHFA: Non-distressed	Assessor: **Distressed** FHFA: **Distressed**	Assessor: Non-distressed FHFA: **Distressed**	Assessor: **Distressed** FHFA: Non-distressed
Miami				
2011q1	27.3%	-4.0%	-2.7%	30.3%
2011q2	22.6%	-6.0%	-2.1%	8.6%
2011q3	21.3%	-26.0%	-1.8%	-14.3%
2011q4	21.3%	-11.9%	-3.1%	-2.7%
Tampa				
2011q1	23.0%	-15.7%	-5.1%	-6.1%
2011q2	19.6%	-19.6%	-9.6%	10.6%
2011q3	13.1%	-5.4%	-18.0%	4.1%
2011q4	11.0%	-25.2%	-11.9%	1.5%
Other Areas in Florida				
2011q1	12.5%	-22.7%	-14.9%	-2.7%
2011q2	10.6%	-24.4%	-17.2%	-6.9%
2011q3	8.8%	-21.2%	-16.0%	-4.9%
2011q4	8.3%	-17.8%	-18.0%	-8.2%

Notes: Transactions data are available in both county recorder data licensed from DataQuick Information Systems as well as county assessment records. Both data sources have relatively complete data coverage (i.e., almost all transactions occurring in the state are reflected in the data), but there are cases where only one source reports a given transaction. Before statistics were computed, transactions that appeared in only one source were removed from the sample.

Sources: County recorder data licensed from DataQuick Information Systems, county assessment records from FDOR and DataQuick Information Systems, mortgage performance information for FHA-endorsed properties supplied by FHA, mortgage performance data for Enterprise-guaranteed loans from the Enterprises' "Historical Loan Performance" dataset, and pre-foreclosure data licensed from CoreLogic.

regression error systemically differs from zero. Recall that the regression error indicates how much the observed price change differs from the market appreciation for a given home over a specific interval. The regression error should be negative when the most recent transaction is a distressed sale. The extent to which it is negative provides information about (a) the accuracy of the identification methodology and (b) the magnitude of the distressed sale discount.

Table 1 presents quarterly average regressions errors for Miami, Tampa, and all other areas in Florida during 2011 (a period when house prices began to rise). The columns provide an opportunity to contrast between the distressed sale indicators. The most recent transaction is the basis for the analysis; the different columns indicate whether there is agreement or disagreement as to whether the most recent transaction in a transaction pair is a distressed sale.[9] Consistent with ex-

---

[9]For ease of interpretation, the regression errors are taken from the first stage of the HPI estimation where the

pectations, the first column—where neither the FHFA nor FDOR indicate a distressed sale—has positive errors. This means that appreciation rates tend to be above average when the most recent transaction is clearly a nondistressed sale. The second column—where both sources concur that the recent sale is distressed—has negative regression errors (appreciation is lower than average). The last two columns are testaments to how well the FHFA and FDOR identification approaches stand on their own. The third column, with the FHFA indicators, has all negative signs and the magnitudes are often half the size as listed in the second column (where both sources concur on the distressed nature). A surprising result appears in the last column. The assessor indicators in the fourth column elicit a mix of negative and positive values with wide fluctuations in absolute magnitudes. While they do have consistently negative values for all other areas in Florida, the absolute magnitudes are quite small compared to the second and third columns.

Based on this table and the prior figure, it seems that the FHFA dataset's distressed sales indicator captures more distressed sales than are identified in the FDOR data. The FDOR's distressed sales indicator performs fine when it concurs with the FHFA data but results are questionable, at best, when the indicator disagrees (the last column).[10] The results in the second column also conform loosely with distressed sale discounts observed in prior literature.

Although they provide some insights, average regression errors do not measure directly the size of the distressed sale discount. This can be achieved by placing indicator variables in the standard repeat sales regression model. The coefficients of such variables can be interpreted as the distressed sale discount.

A crude approach is to insert a single distress variable that takes a value of one when a property's

---

magnitude can be interpreted as the percentage change from the prior sale.

[10]The FDOR is required statutorily to perform random sample tests of sales qualification codes on transacted properties as part of its regulatory review of assessment rolls (*F.S.* 195.0995). Even so, the statute only charges that the code should have a documented reason for disqualifications and does not require the agency to verify the accuracy of other assessor codes, like those associated with distressed sales. The limited oversight may be a reason why the fourth column does not return negative errors consistently.

current sale is flagged as distressed, a negative one when the prior sale is flagged as distressed, and a zero otherwise.[11] This variable acts as a fixed effect, adding or subtracting a calibrated discount where one of the two transactions in the transaction pair are distressed. The single-variable approach assumes that the distressed sale discount remains the same over time. To allow the distressed sale discount to vary over time, a more flexible variant of the crude approach is to interact the distressed sale controls with the time dummy variables. The coefficients on these interactive terms then act as time-specific measures of the distressed sale discount.

While an improvement, the time-specific distress discounts still do not allow the discount to vary depending on whether the distressed sale is the current or the prior sale. Comparing two price pairs, one where a "normal" sale follows a distressed sale and one where a distressed sale follows a normal sale, one might wonder whether the distress discount should necessarily be the same in both cases. For example, if a "stigma" effect exists and appreciation rates are persistently lower when a home is sold previously in a distressed situation, then the discount associated with the prior sale might be lower than a current sale.[12] As with the crude approach, this complicated approach can measure the discount as a fixed effect or as time-specific. [13]

What are reasonable expectations for the distressed sales discount? Based on the regression errors in Table 1, it would seem that the crude approach would likely yield a fixed effect between -10 and -30 percent. The variation between the rows suggests that the distressed discounts should be allowed to vary over time in both the crude and complicated models; distressed discounts seem to have systematically changed as markets have recovered.

---

[11]The value is also set to zero in the very rare cases where both the current and prior sale are distressed sales.

[12]Other than stigma, home quality related issues may also hamper price growth in such cases. Homeowners who have gone into financial distress may allow property condition to lag. Poor maintenance or other quality degradation that occurs in connection with the distress could have persistent effects on long-term price growth.

[13]The methods can be complicated further by distinguishing between properties that have a distressed flag in both the current and prior sale (or even more frequently). However, such advancements may not be a worthy pursuit for multiple reasons: less than 3 percent of paired transactions in any quarter fall into this category, many of the time-varying estimated coefficients are insignificant, and the results mimic what can already be shown with a simpler approach.

Figure 3: Distressed Sales Discounts in Florida using FHFA data

(a) Standard Repeat Sales Approach (Crude)

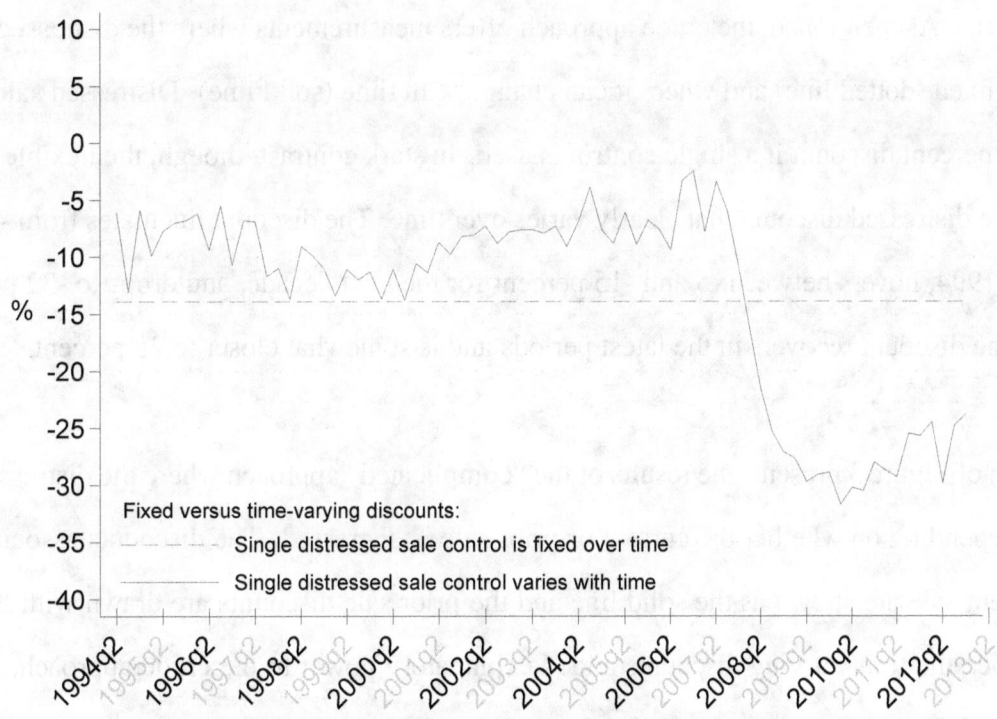

Sources: FHFA, DataQuick Information Systems, FHA, and CoreLogic.

(b) Separation of the Distressed Flag (Complicated)

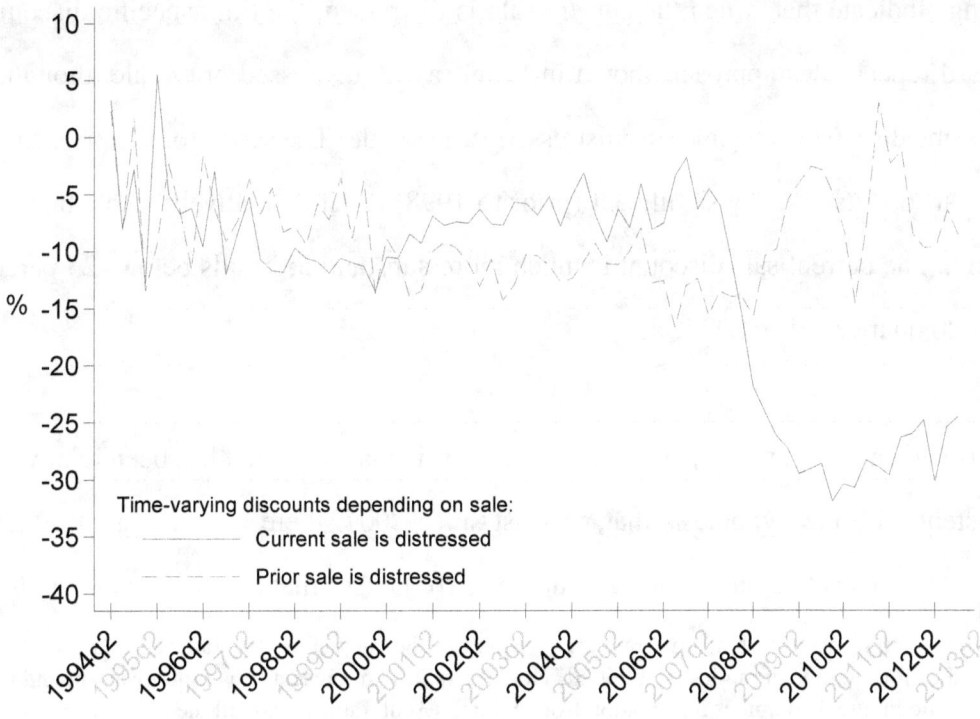

Sources FHFA, DataQuick Information Systems, FHA, and CoreLogic.

Figure 3 graphs the results from regression estimations that incorporate the distressed sale indicators.[14] The figure is split between the crude approaches in Panel (a) and the complicated approach in Panel (b). As mentioned, the crude approach offers measurements where the distressed sale discount is fixed (dotted line) and where it can change with time (solid line). Distressed sales bring a fixed 14 percent discount if a single control is used. In stark contrast, though, the flexible variation portrays a distressed discount that clearly varies over time. The discount fluctuates from -6 percent in early 1994, hovers between -5 and -15 percent for the next decade, and drops to -32 percent by 2010. The discount recovers in the latest periods and is somewhat closer to 25 percent.

Panel (b) of Figure 3 presents the results of the "complicated" approach where the distress discount varies depending on whether the current or prior sale is distressed. The discounts associated with the current sale are shown as the solid line and the prior sale discounts are drawn with the dotted line. Since the time-varying discounts added explanatory power to the crude approach, Panel (b) focuses only on time-varying results for the current sale and prior sale discounts.

The findings indicate that, when the current sale is distressed, the time-specific discount mimics the standard repeat sales approach shown in Panel (a). A distressed prior sale, though, does not carry the same discount over time as a distressed current sale. The series for the prior sale discount does not start out statistically significant (prior to 1998) but it is relatively stable between -3 and -13 percent. The current sale discount is much more substantial; it falls below -25 percent for 15 of the last 20 quarters since 2007Q4.

The results shown in Figure 3—particularly that the prior sale discount has been relatively small—are consistent with the hypothesis that, at least since 2007, there may a stigma effect or some quality-related effects that have hindered outcomes for houses that previously sold in distress. For

---

[14]Numerical coefficients and standard errors are provided in the supplementary Tables 2 and 3 at the end of this paper. Estimates for the time dummies are omitted. Note the tables are presented as time-invariant and time-specific estimations while Figure 3 combines information from column (3) of Table 2 with all the columns in Table 3.

those properties, lower subsequent price gains are observed (i.e, the measured "prior sale" distress discounts are relatively small). The results in the panels are also consistent with an alternative hypothesis: that there is much greater uncertainty over a house's current value when it has not sold previously in distress. With a previously distressed property, the buyer may have a sense for the "downside risk" associated with purchasing that property and, thus, may not command as great of a discount than would otherwise be sought.

V Discussion and Conclusion

The intent of this paper is to break away from the prior research that focuses on individual house prices and to explore how distressed sales affect overall index levels. To that degree, several notable contributions are made. First, HPI trends have clear visual disparities when distressed sales are removed from full samples. Second, the source of data is crucial: the share of distressed sales is several times larger in recent years when public records are complemented with proprietary and private datasets. Third, empirical estimates convey that the distressed sale discount is not fixed—it varies across time and place. The discounts even change depending on whether properties currently or previously receive the distressed sale label. Finally, a method is provided to identify distressed sales and quantify their discounts.

These results should be interpreted with a couple of *caveats* in mind. First, the findings are contingent upon place. This exercise focuses entirely on Florida because public records are standardized and available for a substantial period. Other states and MSAs that experienced a less dramatic crash or fewer distressed sales could show different outcomes.[15] Second, as housing markets are only recently beginning to improve, it is not certain the paper's findings will hold in markets with consistent or rapidly increasing price appreciation. Third, as indicated earlier, comparisons be-

---

[15]A recent working paper by Depken et al. (2013) uses a proxy estimation to measure the discount from foreclosures and distressed sales in Las Vegas when distressed sale indicators are not available. Bourassa et al. (2013) have developed a way to possibly avoid the indicators altogether. Future comparisons with these approaches could provide insights about methodological tradeoffs and how well proxy estimations and robust estimations work in other markets.

tween the FHFA and FDOR distress flags are not possible for periods earlier than 2009 (the FDOR data did not track distressed sales until that year). Although distressed sales occur infrequently farther back in time, it is theoretically possible that—if earlier data were available—some of the paper's findings might differ after incorporating additional data into the analysis.

Future studies of distressed sales could continue in several directions. For instance, this study does not fully address the mechanism by which the distressed sale indicator affects property values and, by extension, the house price indexes. As suggested, distress might carry a negative stigma that affects values or, alternatively, poor property conditions may explain the discounts. The popular press has attributed both problems to the distressed sale discount. This study also leaves open the question of why the regression error is much smaller for the public record data (i.e., the distressed sales only identified by the FDOR data) and whether similar results might be found in other states.

Distressed sales are a sort of abnormality in a well-functioning housing market—they are not the typical arms-length transaction and they represent only a subset of non-qualified sales transactions. Prior studies on house prices had the flexibility of either dropping those observations or completely ignoring their presence. As a result of historically strong house price appreciation and a previously low frequency of distressed sales, the research literature has been silent on the effect of omitting (or not) such observations. In addition, little has been done to compare how distressed sales are identified across data sources. This study has bridged those gaps.

HPIs are used regularly by a variety of people (e.g. investors, realtors, homeowners, insurers, and reporters) who are concerned about real estate values. Indexes are one way to measure changes in the value of such assets and this study has shown that FHFA's purchase-only index HPI has been affected by discounts associated with distressed sales. As housing markets recover, the direction and magnitude of the discounts will remain an important consideration for policy makers and researchers. Overall, this paper provides new insights into the consequences of distressed sales on

HPIs and encourages interested persons to contemplate carefully which types of HPIs they select.

References

Bailey, M. J., Muth, R. F., & Nourse, H. O. (1963). A regression method for real estate price index construction. *Journal of the American Statistical Association*, *58*, 933–942.

Bourassa, S. C., Cantoni, E., & Hoesli, M. (2013). Robust repeat sales indexes. *Real Estate Economics*, forthcoming.

Calhoun, C. A. (1996). OFHEO house price indexes: HPI technical description. Tech. rep., Office of Federal Housing Enterprise Oversight, Washington, DC. From http://www.fhfa.gov/PolicyProgramsResearch/Research/Pages/HPI-Technical-Description.aspx, Staff Working Papers.

Campbell, J. Y., Giglio, S., & Pathak, P. (2011). Forced sales and house prices. *American Economics Review*, *101*, 2108–2131.

Case, K. E. & Shiller, R. J. (1987). Prices of single family homes since 1970: New indexes for four cities. *New England Economic Review*, 45–56.

Case, K. E. & Shiller, R. J. (1989). The efficiency of the market for single-family homes. *American Economic Review*, *79*, 125–137.

Depken, C. A., Hollans, H., & Swidler, S. (2013). A low cost methodology for correcting the distressed sales bias in a downward spiraling housing market. Working Paper.

Federal Housing Finance Agency (2012a). Distress-free house price indexes. Tech. rep., Washington, DC. From http://www.fhfa.gov/DataTools/Downloads/Documents/HPI_Focus_Pieces/2012Q2_HPIFocus_N508.pdf, Quarterly Highlights Piece.

Federal Housing Finance Agency (2012b). Options for constructing "distress-free" house price indexes. Tech. rep., Washington, DC. From http://www.fhfa.gov/DataTools/Downloads/Documents/HPI_Focus_Pieces/2012Q1_HPIFocus_N508.pdf, Quarterly Highlights Piece.

Federal Housing Finance Agency (2012c). A primer on price discount of Real Estate Owned (REO) properties. Tech. rep., Washington, DC. From http://www.fhfa.gov/PolicyProgramsResearch/Research/Pages/Mortgage-Market-Note-12-01.aspx, Mortgage Market Note 12-01.

Gatzlaff, D. H. & Ling, D. C. (1994). Measuring changes in local house prices: An empirical investigation of alternative methodologies. *Journal of Urban Economics*, *35*, 221–244.

Harding, J. P., Rosenblatt, E., & Yao, V. W. (2009). The contagion effect of foreclosed properties. *Journal of Urban Economics*, *66*, 164–178.

Harding, J. P., Rosenblatt, E., & Yao, V. W. (2012). The foreclosure discount: Myth or reality? *Journal of Urban Economics*, *71*, 204–218.

Immergluck, D. & Smith, G. (2006). The external costs of foreclosure: The impact of single-family mortgage foreclosures on property values. *Housing Policy Debate*, *17*, 57–79.

Linneman, P. (1980). Some empirical results on the nature of the hedonic price function for the urban housing market. *Journal of Urban Economics*, *8*, 47–68.

Noeth, B. & Sengupta, R. (2011). A closer look at house price indexes. Tech. rep., St. Louis Fed. From `http://www.stlouisfed.org/publications/re/articles/?id=2126`.

Rosen, S. (1974). Hedonic prices and implicit markets: Product differentiation in pure competition. *Journal of Political Economy*, *82*, 34–55.

Sirmans, C. F. & Slade, B. A. (2012). National transaction-based land price indices. *Journal of Real Estate Finance and Economics*, *45*, 829–845.

Sirmans, G. S., MacDonald, L., Macpherson, D. A., & Zietz, E. N. (2006). The value of housing characteristics: A meta analysis. *Journal of Real Estate Finance and Economics*, *33*, 215–240.

Towe, C. & Lawley, C. (2013). The contagion effect of neighborhood foreclosures. *American Economic Journal: Economic Policy*, *5*, 313–335.

Table 2: Estimations with Distressed Identifiers as Time-Invariant Dummy Variables (across Florida from 1994Q1 to 2012Q4)

Estimation	Standard Repeat Sales Approach (Crude)						Separation of the Distressed Flag (Complicated)					
	(1) Multiple Flags		(2) Single Flag		(3) Single FHFA Flag		(4) Multiple Flags		(5) Single Flag		(6) Single FHFA Flag	
	Coefficient	S.E.	Coefficient	S.E.	Coefficient	S.E.	Coefficient	S.E.	Coefficient	S.E.	Coefficient	S.E.
Either Sale is Distressed												
Assessor and FHFA	-0.304***	(0.005)										
Assessor	-0.090***	(0.006)										
FHFA	-0.133***	(0.002)			-0.141***	(0.002)						
Assessor, FHFA, or both			-0.141***	(0.002)								
Current Sale												
Assessor and FHFA							-0.308***	(0.005)				
Assessor							-0.093***	(0.006)				
FHFA							-0.143***	(0.002)			-0.153***	(0.002)
Assessor, FHFA, or both									-0.152***	(0.002)		
Prior Sale												
Assessor and FHFA							-0.266***	(0.034)				
FHFA							-0.103***	(0.037)			-0.109***	(0.003)
Assessor							-0.108***	(0.003)				
Assessor, FHFA, or both									-0.109***	(0.003)		
$\sqrt{MSE}$	0.250		0.251		0.251		0.250		0.251		0.251	
Adjusted R^2	0.796		0.795		0.795		0.796		0.795		0.795	

Note: Calculations are performed for the entire state of Florida using the FHFA and assessor (FDOR) distressed indicators on properties as indicated in the variable names. The base comparison for the "varying by flag" estimations is that neither source indicates distressed. The only level of statistical significance shown is *** for $p = 0.01$.
Sources: FHFA, DataQuick Information Systems, FHA, and CoreLogic.

Table 3: Estimations with Distressed Identifiers as Time-Specific Dummy Variables (across Florida from 1994Q1 to 2012Q4)

| | | Standard Repeat Sales (Crude) | | Separation of the Distressed Flag (Complicated) | | | |
| | | (1) Either Sale is Distressed | | (2) Current Sale | | (3) Prior Sale | |
Year	Quarter	Coefficient	S.E.	Coefficient	S.E.	Coefficient	S.E.
1994	1	—	—	—	—	—	—
1994	2	-0.061**	(0.024)	0.033	(0.049)	0.023	(0.113)
1994	3	-0.131***	(0.025)	-0.080	(0.057)	-0.081	(0.103)
1994	4	-0.059**	(0.026)	-0.028	(0.067)	0.017	(0.126)
1995	1	-0.099***	(0.024)	-0.128**	(0.050)	-0.134	(0.125)
1995	2	-0.077***	(0.022)	0.055	(0.043)	-0.094	(0.077)
1995	3	-0.070***	(0.022)	-0.050	(0.035)	-0.023	(0.061)
1995	4	-0.068***	(0.019)	-0.067**	(0.031)	-0.065	(0.069)
1996	1	-0.062***	(0.020)	-0.062**	(0.031)	-0.116	(0.075)
1996	2	-0.094***	(0.018)	-0.096***	(0.028)	-0.016	(0.052)
1996	3	-0.055***	(0.018)	-0.029	(0.027)	-0.062	(0.069)
1996	4	-0.107***	(0.019)	-0.120***	(0.028)	-0.091*	(0.051)
1997	1	-0.068***	(0.020)	-0.084***	(0.028)	-0.073	(0.061)
1997	2	-0.069***	(0.018)	-0.052**	(0.025)	-0.036	(0.053)
1997	3	-0.117***	(0.015)	-0.107***	(0.022)	-0.067	(0.053)
1997	4	-0.110***	(0.016)	-0.117***	(0.021)	-0.044	(0.041)
1998	1	-0.137***	(0.016)	-0.118***	(0.021)	-0.083*	(0.048)
1998	2	-0.091***	(0.014)	-0.097***	(0.020)	-0.078**	(0.038)
1998	3	-0.099***	(0.014)	-0.106***	(0.018)	-0.094***	(0.033)
1998	4	-0.110***	(0.013)	-0.109***	(0.016)	-0.058*	(0.032)
1999	1	-0.134***	(0.014)	-0.119***	(0.018)	-0.072**	(0.036)
1999	2	-0.111***	(0.013)	-0.106***	(0.017)	-0.035	(0.030)
1999	3	-0.120***	(0.013)	-0.110***	(0.017)	-0.089***	(0.033)
1999	4	-0.113***	(0.013)	-0.113***	(0.017)	-0.038	(0.032)
2000	1	-0.137***	(0.014)	-0.135***	(0.018)	-0.137***	(0.032)
2000	2	-0.111***	(0.013)	-0.105***	(0.016)	-0.089***	(0.026)
2000	3	-0.138***	(0.013)	-0.106***	(0.017)	-0.106***	(0.026)
2000	4	-0.106***	(0.012)	-0.085***	(0.015)	-0.140***	(0.025)
2001	1	-0.114***	(0.012)	-0.093***	(0.016)	-0.135***	(0.027)

Continued on next page

Year	Quarter	Either Sale is Distressed		Current Sale		Prior Sale	
2001	2	-0.087***	(0.011)	-0.069***	(0.015)	-0.100***	(0.021)
2001	3	-0.098***	(0.011)	-0.077***	(0.014)	-0.092***	(0.021)
2001	4	-0.082***	(0.011)	-0.074***	(0.014)	-0.097***	(0.021)
2002	1	-0.081***	(0.012)	-0.075***	(0.014)	-0.110***	(0.022)
2002	2	-0.073***	(0.010)	-0.063***	(0.013)	-0.131***	(0.018)
2002	3	-0.088***	(0.010)	-0.076***	(0.014)	-0.107***	(0.019)
2002	4	-0.078***	(0.010)	-0.077***	(0.012)	-0.143***	(0.017)
2003	1	-0.076***	(0.011)	-0.057***	(0.013)	-0.129***	(0.019)
2003	2	-0.076***	(0.010)	-0.058***	(0.013)	-0.103***	(0.016)
2003	3	-0.079***	(0.010)	-0.068***	(0.012)	-0.104***	(0.016)
2003	4	-0.073***	(0.011)	-0.052***	(0.013)	-0.112***	(0.017)
2004	1	-0.091***	(0.012)	-0.078***	(0.014)	-0.127***	(0.017)
2004	2	-0.069***	(0.012)	-0.051***	(0.014)	-0.124***	(0.015)
2004	3	-0.039***	(0.012)	-0.031**	(0.014)	-0.109***	(0.017)
2004	4	-0.076***	(0.013)	-0.068***	(0.015)	-0.093***	(0.018)
2005	1	-0.088***	(0.014)	-0.092***	(0.016)	-0.111***	(0.018)
2005	2	-0.061***	(0.014)	-0.063***	(0.016)	-0.112***	(0.015)
2005	3	-0.089***	(0.015)	-0.079***	(0.017)	-0.100***	(0.016)
2005	4	-0.068***	(0.017)	-0.041**	(0.019)	-0.079***	(0.019)
2006	1	-0.076***	(0.019)	-0.081***	(0.021)	-0.128***	(0.020)
2006	2	-0.094***	(0.017)	-0.075***	(0.020)	-0.126***	(0.017)
2006	3	-0.033*	(0.019)	-0.034	(0.021)	-0.167***	(0.021)
2006	4	-0.025	(0.019)	-0.018	(0.021)	-0.130***	(0.021)
2007	1	-0.078***	(0.017)	-0.063***	(0.019)	-0.124***	(0.020)
2007	2	-0.034**	(0.014)	-0.045***	(0.014)	-0.156***	(0.017)
2007	3	-0.061***	(0.013)	-0.060***	(0.013)	-0.135***	(0.018)
2007	4	-0.110***	(0.011)	-0.106***	(0.012)	-0.140***	(0.019)
2008	1	-0.165***	(0.012)	-0.156***	(0.012)	-0.140***	(0.023)
2008	2	-0.216***	(0.011)	-0.219***	(0.011)	-0.157***	(0.023)
2008	3	-0.253***	(0.011)	-0.241***	(0.012)	-0.104***	(0.025)
2008	4	-0.271***	(0.012)	-0.262***	(0.012)	-0.098***	(0.030)
2009	1	-0.277***	(0.013)	-0.273***	(0.013)	-0.054	(0.034)
2009	2	-0.297***	(0.012)	-0.295***	(0.012)	-0.039	(0.029)
2009	3	-0.291***	(0.012)	-0.291***	(0.012)	-0.026	(0.030)
2009	4	-0.289***	(0.012)	-0.286***	(0.012)	-0.029	(0.028)
2010	1	-0.317***	(0.014)	-0.319***	(0.014)	-0.051	(0.037)

Continued on next page

Year	Quarter	Either Sale is Distressed		Current Sale		Prior Sale	
2010	2	-0.302***	(0.012)	-0.304***	(0.012)	-0.083***	(0.028)
2010	3	-0.305***	(0.013)	-0.307***	(0.013)	-0.146***	(0.031)
2010	4	-0.280***	(0.013)	-0.283***	(0.013)	-0.073**	(0.030)
2011	1	-0.287***	(0.013)	-0.289***	(0.013)	0.031	(0.030)
2011	2	-0.293***	(0.012)	-0.296***	(0.012)	-0.023	(0.029)
2011	3	-0.255***	(0.012)	-0.263***	(0.012)	-0.012	(0.026)
2011	4	-0.257***	(0.013)	-0.260***	(0.013)	-0.085***	(0.028)
2012	1	-0.245***	(0.014)	-0.248***	(0.014)	-0.097***	(0.033)
2012	2	-0.298***	(0.013)	-0.302***	(0.013)	-0.096***	(0.026)
2012	3	-0.248***	(0.012)	-0.254***	(0.012)	-0.064***	(0.025)
2012	4	-0.238***	(0.014)	-0.245***	(0.014)	-0.087***	(0.026)
$\sqrt{MSE}$		0.249				0.249	
Adjusted R^2		0.798				0.798	

Note: Calculations are performed for the entire state of Florida using only the FHFA distressed indicators on properties. To conserve space, the variables used in each regression estimation are presented as separate columns. Unique estimations are indicated in the subtitles that merge across columns. The levels of statistical significance are defined as * for $p = .10$, ** for $p = .05$, and *** for $p = 0.01$.
Sources: FHFA, DataQuick Information Systems, FHA, and CoreLogic.